BECOME AN EXPERT
JOKE-TELLER

Published in 2020 by Write Laugh Books
Rotorua, New Zealand

Text © Tom E. Moffatt, 2020

Illustrations © Paul Beavis, 2020

www.tomemoffatt.com

ISBN: 978-0-9951210-4-1 (print)
ISBN: 978-0-9951210-5-8 (e-book)

A catalogue record for this book is available from the National Library of New Zealand.

Cover design and illustrations: Paul Beavis
Developmental and copy editing: Anna Bowles
Proofreading: Marj Griffiths, Rainbow Resolutions
Print book and e-book design: Write Laugh Books

BECOME AN EXPERT
JOKE-TELLER

★

TOM E. MOFFATT

★

ILLUSTRATED BY
PAUL BEAVIS

To Sarah...

because being married to me is no joke!

★ CONTENTS ★

Introduction..................................... 7

How to Use this Book......................13

Types of Jokes 15

Know Your Joke 27

Exercise 1 37

Know Your Audience 42

Exercise 2 54

The Delivery 59

Exercise 3 67

Right Time, Right Place 74

Exercise 4 82

Joke-telling Sessions......................87

Exercise 5 98

Go with the Flow 106

Exercise 6 115

Build Your Repertoire 125

Exercise 7 136

Longer Jokes 143

Exercise 8 158

The Beginning 175

Also by Tom E. Moffatt 178

About the Author 183

Resources 184

Acknowledgements 185

★ **INTRODUCTION** ★

Some people make a living from writing jokes and comedy. These people, known as comedians or stand-up comedians, write and perform comedy shows and routines. Other people, such as that popular kid in your class or your slightly annoying uncle, just enjoy telling jokes to friends and family.

This casual form of joke-telling is the focus of this book. Those moments when someone tells a joke in the playground or at a party, and before the laughter has entirely stopped, someone else chips in with another. Suddenly we're in one of those special joke-telling moments, where everybody is racking their brains for the perfect next joke that will have everyone in stitches.

Some people thrive in these situations. They seem to have a limitless supply of jokes that they deliver confidently and effortlessly to continued laughter. These days, I probably fall into this category. I have written hundreds of original jokes and people know this. When a joke-telling situation arises, all eyes invariably turn to me. And I am usually happy to oblige.

But this wasn't always the case.

Like many kids, I used to love joke books. I'd request them for birthdays and Christmas, and read them aloud to anyone who would listen. But I was terrible at joke-telling.

I could never remember any once I'd put the book down and I was painfully shy, so my efforts were barely audible. Even when the joke could be heard, I'd often muddle it up and say the punchline first, finding myself in that lonely laughter-free zone found at the end of a badly told joke.

That didn't stop me from loving jokes. And I was fortunate enough to be surrounded by many excellent joke-tellers. My older brother, my friends at school, my granddad. I enjoyed hearing jokes so much that I started to collect them, writing them down in a large notebook. I'd tell them to myself when I had down time, running through all my favourites and often giggling at the punchlines. But I was still very nervous when I had to share jokes with anyone else.

It wasn't until I was travelling the world, meeting different people every day and finding endless opportunities to practise my jokes, that I began to develop my skills.

INTRODUCTION

My confidence grew and I started remembering all the jokes I'd collected over the years. Suddenly, I found myself loving the limelight. I'd initiate joke-telling sessions whenever I could and continued to gather fresh jokes for my collection. I eventually began writing my own jokes, too.

This just goes to show that joke-telling is a skill. And like all skills, it can be mastered with practice. If you read through the tips in this book, memorise some of the jokes and practise telling them, you will develop that skill. It won't happen overnight. But with a little effort, you'll find yourself looking forward to the next spontaneous joke-telling session.

And when you're in the midst of it, you'll wait for that pause in the laughter. You'll say, "I've got one..." There'll be a moment's silence while your audience looks your way, hoping to hear a well-told joke that they can pass on to others. But, more importantly, hoping to laugh.

And you won't disappoint.

★ HOW TO USE ★ THIS BOOK

You're Joking: Become an Expert Joke-teller is more than just a joke book.

It's an instruction manual that also provides you with 101 jokes to hone your skills. Each section contains basic tips and information, followed by practice jokes and exercises, and ending with a reflection. The jokes are numbered from 1 to 101, so you can jot down the number, rather than the whole thing.

As with regular joke books, you can dip in and out as you please, sharing funny jokes when you discover them. However, the instructional tips and exercises build on each other, so you will get the most from this book if you read it from start to finish. This is not a school assignment, so you don't need to complete every single exercise if you don't want to. But practice makes perfect, so the more you use this book to help you practise, the closer you will get to becoming an expert joke-teller.

★ TYPES OF JOKES ★

WHAT IS A JOKE?

This might sound like a bit of a stupid question, but jokes actually come in many shapes and disguises.

In its basic form, a joke is something you say to make someone laugh. It's generally made up of two parts – the setup and the punchline. The setup introduces the topic and leads the audience in one direction. The punchline (or punch) is a short delivery that changes the direction of the joke and gives the audience a surprise, hopefully making them laugh at the same time.

DIFFERENT TYPES OF JOKES

There are many types of jokes and humour. Enough, in fact, to fill several books. We are only going to focus on the kinds that you might hear in the playground or read in a joke book.

ONE-LINERS

The shortest joke is the one-liner, where both the setup and the punch are delivered in a single statement, usually within one or two sentences. A joke of this kind takes on the appearance of an ordinary statement or observation, until the punch turns it on its head.

1. I wondered why the football was getting bigger and bigger. And then it hit me.

2. Diarrhoea is hereditary. It runs in your jeans.

3. Statistically speaking, six out of seven dwarfs are not Happy.

QUESTION-AND-ANSWER JOKES

These are the most common jokes in a joke book. The setup comes in the form of a question, and the punchline is the response.

4. **Why can't cats sing in key?**
   They always eat the tuner.

5. **Why do cows wear bells?**
   Because their horns don't work.

6. **What did one eye say to the other eye?**
   Between you and me, there's something that smells.

KNOCK-KNOCK JOKES

While these are technically question-and-answer jokes, their continuing popularity demands a section of their own. As you probably know, a knock-knock joke starts with a person knocking on an imaginary door. The audience – or pretend resident – says *Who's there?* This is when the joke-teller delivers the setup: a name or object that is supposedly at the door. The audience then says, "Name or object *who*?", allowing the joke-teller to hit them with a punchline that usually begins with their chosen name or object.

7. Knock, knock…

Who's there?

Anita…

Anita who?

Anita use your bathroom.

8. **Knock, knock...**

Who's there?

Bean...

Bean who?

**Bean waiting here for ages.
What took you so long?**

LONGER JOKES

Some jokes take on the form of a story, complete with added details and actions. This long setup leads you towards a short, sharp punchline.

9. Little Ghost was so terrible at haunting houses he decided to go back to school to learn how to do it properly. On the first day, the teacher taught the class how to fly through walls. After working on it for nearly an hour, she asked, "Is there anyone who hasn't got the hang of it yet?"

   Nervously, Little Ghost put up his hand.

   "Don't worry," the teacher said. "Look at the whiteboard and I'll go through it again."

SHAGGY DOG STORIES

Beware the shaggy dog story. These take on the appearance of long jokes, except that they use excessive detail to make the 'joke' unnecessarily long. Then, just when you're hoping for an awesome punch to make it all worthwhile, they purposely fail to deliver.

I once heard the following 'joke' told by a friend. While he was telling it, I was rather impressed. I mentally noted down all the key points, so that I could add it to my collection. But then I heard the terrible punchline and no amount of punching myself would make me forget it.

10. One morning, a boy walked into school with an orange for a head. All the kids gathered round him, pointing and laughing.

"What the heck happened?" someone eventually asked.

"Well," said the boy, "it's a pretty funny story. I was rummaging around my garage, looking for parts for a go-cart, when I found this rusty old lamp. I thought it might be worth something if I cleaned it up, so I grabbed an old rag off the bench and gave it a rub. A flash of light filled the room and out popped this wispy little green fellow. In a squeaky voice he said, 'I am the Greenie Genie and I grant you threeeee wishes!'"

"What did you wish for?" someone asked.

"For my first wish, I wished for a bathtub full of ice cream. I ran upstairs to discover the tub was piled high with ice cream of every colour and flavour you could imagine. There was chocolate, caramel, strawberry, banana. Everything. All the colours of the rainbow and more. I didn't even bother to get a spoon. I just stuck my head in and slurped up as much as I could before it started to melt."

"Wow!" the other kids said, staring at him in awe. "Then what did you wish for?"

"After that, I wished for a puppy. And the next thing I knew, the cutest puppy I'd ever seen was yapping away and running around my ankles. We played for ages, rolling around on the carpet and cuddling each other. Then it too discovered the bathtub full of ice cream and started lapping it up."

"And then what happened?"

"At that point I only had one wish left, so I wished I had an orange for a head."

AVOID OFFENSIVE JOKES

Jokes can often be offensive. They can make fun of different nationalities, ethnicities and social groups. They can also contain offensive language or actions. There's no need for this. It's perfectly possible to tell a funny joke that contains no negativity towards individuals or nations and does not cause offence.

For obvious reasons, I won't give an example of an offensive joke. All the jokes in this book are 'clean' and hopefully do not offend any people, animals or inanimate objects. You will, however, find a fair share of bum, poo and fart jokes. While not entirely clean, they cannot be considered offensive unless they contain swearwords or make fun of particular people.

When looking for jokes, try to avoid adult-only sources, since these may contain material that is not suitable for children. If you're searching on the internet, you should write 'for kids' at the end of the search topic, as this will hopefully weed out most inappropriate content. If in doubt, ask an adult to help you.

★ KNOW YOUR JOKE ★

BUILDING A REPERTOIRE

The secret to being an expert joke-teller is knowing lots of jokes. This is not something that happens overnight.

A good joke-teller consciously collects material throughout their lifetime, in the same way that you might collect coins or Pokémon cards. They are always on the lookout for a worthy addition, growing and nurturing their collection whenever they can.

This is called building your repertoire (pronounced REP-er-twar). Like a coin collection, a joke repertoire is never really complete. There is always another yet-to-be-discovered joke that would make a perfect addition to your collection.

The great thing about jokes is that, unlike with lyrics or poetry, they don't need to be memorised word for word. As long as you remember the key points and punchline, you should still get a laugh. Shorter jokes tend to stick more closely to their original version, but with longer jokes, you can add your own details and embellishments. This kind of personalisation helps you build a unique repertoire that is truly your own.

SEARCH FOR JOKES

When starting any collection, you need to actively go looking for new additions. You can't call yourself a coin collector just because you've got the change from a dollar in your pocket. You need to discover several fine specimens, making sure they're polished and well presented.

It's the same with jokes. If the only jokes you know are the ones that do laps of the playground every break time, you won't be any better than the next kid, no matter how well you tell them. You should always be on the lookout for hilarious new jokes. And not just the ones you find funny yourself. Think about your audience and the things that they might laugh at.

Joke books are a great place to start. If it's your book – not a library book – then take a pencil and circle all the jokes that make you laugh or that someone you know might find

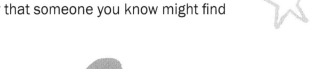

funny. Perhaps search the internet for jokes on different topics. And of course, listen out for good jokes. When you hear someone telling a joke, listen carefully in case it's worth adding to your own repertoire.

WRITE THEM DOWN

Unless your memory is completely airtight – unlike mine – you should consider keeping a joke notebook or online document. Think of it as a place to store your fancy new collection. You wouldn't spend all your pocket money on a rare Roman coin, only to chuck it in your sock drawer, never to be seen again. You'd put it on display, or at the very least, store it with similar coins.

This is what you should do with your jokes. Find yourself an empty journal or exercise book and start writing down all the great jokes that you discover. You can divide them into different categories, either by subject matter or by types of joke. Or you can just write them in order of discovery. Whatever works for you.

You'll probably find that just writing the joke down helps you to remember it better. But even if it doesn't, you'll have the notebook as a place of reference. After a while, flicking through your notebook every now and then will be all you need to do to keep your mental repertoire stocked and ready.

In saying all that, my joke notebook was always a bit of a disaster. It was a large artist's sketchbook with no lines, and my handwriting was so messy that it was like a secret code that only I could decipher – and even I struggled to read it most of the time. I also found it hard to keep organised, jotting each joke down in the first available blank spot. It was virtually impossible to find anything without reading the entire book. However, the advantage of that is I can still remember many of the jokes thirty years later.

These days, I keep all my jokes in a cloud-based document. It's divided into different categories and audiences, and has sections for jokes that I've heard, and ones I've made up, as well as ideas for future jokes. This is synced with all my devices, so it doesn't matter where I am, I can always access my jokes. Rarely does a day go by when I don't visit it to jot something down or remind myself of a particular punchline.

VARIETY

Different people find different things funny.
The wider the variety of jokes in your
collection, the more likely you'll be able to find
the right joke for each situation. Try to include
different types of jokes, from one-liners to
much longer story-jokes, and also vary the
themes and topics of your jokes. This way
you're more likely to know the perfect joke for
each situation and audience.

LEARN YOUR JOKES

A joke notebook, or even a joke book, should never be read aloud. This is not story time. You cannot deliver a joke perfectly, to maximum effect, if you are reading it from the page.

Often, simply flicking through your joke notebook is enough to keep shorter jokes alive in your mind. Another way is to have a silent joke-telling session with yourself, perhaps when you're on a bus or in a queue. Go through all the jokes you can remember, one at a time. Then, when you're back at your joke notebook, have a look to see which ones you forgot.

KNOW YOUR JOKE

With longer jokes you might need to practise them repeatedly to make sure you don't forget anything vital when you're telling the joke. There's nothing worse than arriving at a punchline only to realise you forgot to include a key piece of information earlier on.

You can also practise inside your head when you have some down time. Slowly dissect the joke in your mind, identifying all the crucial elements. Remember that you don't need to memorise it word for word. You can add your own details and descriptions to really take ownership of longer jokes.

I know this all sounds a bit weird, but actors do it all the time. They are always learning their lines and practising them in front of the mirror to get ready for their performance. And joke-telling is just another type of performance, so if you want to be a true expert, you need to get yourself prepared.

THE JOKE COLLECTOR'S NOTEBOOK

If, like me, you find the organisation part difficult, you could try using my Joke Collector's Notebook. This is a journal I have created to make joke collecting easier and more enjoyable. It's divided into different sections, with fun illustrations and handy tips.

You can buy the book version to keep in your sock drawer, or to download a digital copy for free, go to *www.TomEMoffatt.com/notebook*.

★ EXERCISE 1 ★

For your first exercise, you are going to start your written joke collection. Don't worry if you haven't got the perfect notebook yet … you can always copy them over later.

RIGHT NOW, all you need is a few scraps of paper, an old spelling book from Grade One or perhaps a new Google doc.

Here are ten possible entries for your collection. Read through them and choose the funniest few. Don't take them all, though, even if you're easily tickled. This is a collection for your absolute favourites, so pick the top three or four jokes that make you laugh the loudest and add them to your written repertoire.

11. How do the police get rid of flies?

They call the SWAT team.

12. Waking up this morning was an eye-opening experience!

13. What did the plate say to the saucer?

Dinner is on me.

14. What wobbles when it cries?

A jelly baby

15. Which side of a chicken has the most feathers?

The outside

16. I used to be a werewolf, but I'm all right nowoooooooooo!

17. Why didn't the skeleton go to the party?

It had no body to go with.

18. What language do oranges speak?

> Mandarin

19. Which dog has five legs?

> A poorly-trained Rottweiler

20. What's the best way to stop your nose running?

> Trip it up

Did you write down your favourite jokes already?

Well done ... you have started your lifelong joke repertoire! From now on, as you work through the exercises in this book, try to get in the habit of adding your favourites to your collection. Also, every time you hear a joke at school or on TV that makes you laugh – or that you think will make someone you know laugh – jot it down in your collection. And if you're not sure what other people find funny, don't panic! That's what we look at in the next section.

KNOW YOUR AUDIENCE

Jokes are like underpants. There is no one-size-fits-all. You can't buy the same pair of undies for your little sister that you'd buy for your dad. You'd need to know their size and preferred style.

It's the same when you're telling jokes. You have to choose each joke carefully to suit the specific audience. Your choice of jokes for your friends should be very different to the ones you tell your grandmother. In the same way that their choice of underpants is likely to be quite different.

It's not only about age and gender. Everyone has different tastes and preferences, regardless of how old they are. That's what makes us who we are. However, you can make a few generalisations to get you on the right track.

GENERAL RULES FOR KIDS

Younger kids tend to like silly
jokes with very simple wordplay,
often containing toilet humour.
My five-year-old rolls around
in hysterics at the mention
of poo, wee or bums. And
my two-year-old just says
"Poo-poo bum!" at every
available opportunity,
hoping to get a laugh
out of her audience (and often succeeding).

As children get older they enjoy increasingly
complex wordplay and get a kick out of
understanding a joke. My eight-year-old laughs
at many more of my jokes these days and often
says, "Oh, I get it!" while she's laughing. She
still loves toilet humour (as do I!) but is also
keen on general interest topics, such as
animals, sports and school.

In the teenage years, specific interests come into play. A teenager who loves football will enjoy football jokes. One who loves horses will like horsing around. It becomes harder to generalise as we discover who we are and where we fit in the world.

GENERAL RULES FOR ADULTS

When telling jokes to adults, age becomes less important. It's more about the individual's tastes and beliefs. Some people continue to love toilet humour throughout their life. Some find it childish and silly.

Religious beliefs, nationality and social status can often affect our outlook and tastes, but even then, there is always variation from person to person.

NOT SUITABLE FOR ADULTS

Topics such as politics and current affairs are generally appreciated more by adults than by kids. Adults also like jokes requiring specialist knowledge from their interests or fields of expertise, but these can be hard for anyone else to understand.

If in doubt, you can always ask if the other person knows any jokes. You'll be able to tell from their choice of jokes what kind of things they find funny.

Can you think of one joke that you might tell each of these people?

QUICK EXERCISE

Read through the five jokes on the next page. Choose the most appropriate joke for each of the characters below and write its letter in the square.

a. Why did the dog breathe into the washing machine?

It was trying to clean its pants.

b. Teacher: "Why are you talking during my lesson?"

Student: Why are you teaching during my conversation?"

c. How are stars like false teeth?

They both come out at night!

d. What's the difference between the England football team and a tea bag?

The tea bag stays in the cup longer

e. Why did the toilet paper roll down the hill?

It wanted to get to the bottom.

I DON'T GET IT!

We've established that you need to choose jokes about subjects that interest your audience. But also, if you want them to laugh, your audience must understand the joke. There's nothing worse than telling an utterly hilarious joke to someone, only for them to stare at you blankly and say, "I don't get it!". Nothing makes a joke less funny than having to explain why it is funny.

Young children will not understand jokes that contain obscure words or phrases. Equally, people just learning English will struggle with jokes containing complicated language play. Therefore, simple vocabulary and lots of actions work better with these audiences.

Regional slang and cultural concepts do not travel well, either. Using the words guff, grot or dosh outside the UK will cause confusion. As would Cattywampus or podunk if you exported them from the US. And depending on where you are when you tell a joke about football, you might need to clarify whether you mean soccer or gridiron.

When I was backpacking around the world, I often found myself in joke-telling situations. It didn't take too many blank stares before I realised I needed to revise my repertoire. I started collecting jokes that relied more on actions and universal truths than on language play, and before long had the perfect collection for a global, non-native audience.

COMMON THEMES

Sometimes a particular audience will have shared interests or understandings that you can use in your jokes. For example, when you're at school you can be fairly certain that jokes about teachers will be understood by everyone. Similarly, people at your ballet class or football club will enjoy jokes on those themes.

Dual language jokes work very well in parts of the world, too. If everyone has a reasonable understanding of a second language, then why not include both languages within a joke? When I lived in Japan, I collected a trusty repertoire of jokes in Japanese that all used little snippets of English in the punchline and they always (or nearly always) went down well with both locals and foreigners.

PLAY IT SAFE

If you don't know the audience very well, it's
best to play it safe. Have a collection of clean,
universal jokes that work in any situation.
These can be your bread-and-butter jokes that
you use while you're sizing up your audience.

This is a lesson I learnt the hard way. I
recently turned up to a party and was
introduced as Tom who writes funny stories
and jokes for kids. The moment I sat down the

older man next to me said, "You write jokes, eh? Tell us one!"

That's a sure-fire way to make my mind go blank. I've written hundreds of jokes, but the only ones I could think of were the bum jokes I'd been working on that week. The first one to pop out of my mouth was a rather naughty joke about our souls in heaven.

The guy stared back at me, his face expressionless with not a smile or giggle in sight. I quickly moved on to a few of my reliable dog and cat jokes, which fortunately got some laughs. Only later, once the conversation had developed, did I learn that the man was a vicar.

★ EXERCISE 2 ★

Here are ten more jokes. When you read through them, get in the habit of adding the best ones to your joke notebook. Once you've done that, go on to the exercise that follows.

21. **Why do French people eat snails?**

    They don't like fast food.

22. **What can you put in a bucket to make it lighter?**

    A hole

23. Two elephants fall off a cliff...

Boom, boom.

24. Why did the bum get a slap?

It was being cheeky.

25. I can't stand Russian dolls. They're so full of themselves.

26. Why did the baby cookie crumble?

Its mum was a wafer so long.

27. **Therapist:** Your wife says you never buy her flowers. Is this true?

    My dad: To be honest, I never knew she sold flowers.

28. What did the old dog say to its bone?

    It's been nice gnawing you.

29. Thanks for explaining the word 'many' to me ... it means a lot.

30. Why did the idiot have brown hair?

    He made his own shampoo.

For your first joke-telling practice, I'd like you to try a few jokes on someone today.

It could be a sister or brother, a parent or guardian. It doesn't matter. What matters is that you know them well enough to understand the kinds of jokes they find funny.

Once you have chosen your target audience, write their name down below. Then read through the jokes in this section again, choosing the three jokes you think that person will like the most and write the joke numbers beside their name.

Note: You can also use jokes from the previous section, if you think some of those are more suitable.

Name:		
Joke 1	Joke 2	Joke 3

Before you rush off to tell them, read your selected jokes several times, memorising them as well as you can. When you're confident that you know them sufficiently, go and tell the jokes. Don't be tempted to keep going until you've told them every joke in this book. Keep it at three. You can try other jokes out on them later.

Good luck, and I'll see you when you get back.

REFLECTION

How did that go? Don't panic if you didn't get any laughs at all. Maybe you should rethink the kinds of jokes that person likes. Or it might be that you need to improve your joke-telling skills. We'll work on that in the next section.

★ THE DELIVERY ★

There are a few things you need to get right when delivering your jokes. I've already mentioned that you should never read jokes out, but just memorising the words is not enough.

You could have the funniest joke in the world, but if you deliver it badly, no one will laugh. So you need to practise your delivery until you can tell it perfectly. A well-told joke can have the audience laughing before you get to the punchline, which is exactly what you want. Below are some of the elements to focus on when telling a joke.

EYE CONTACT

Look at your audience when you tell your joke.
If it's one person, look them directly in the eye.
If it's more than one, look from person to
person as you move through the joke. If you
appear confident in your telling, you're more
likely to get people laughing. And eye contact
is one of the best ways to show confidence.

THE DELIVERY

SMILE

Another way to portray confidence in your joke is to smile while you tell it. It shows your audience that you like your joke and gets them anticipating the punchline. What you don't want to do is laugh while you're telling your joke, especially not at the end. Nothing signifies a failed joke more than only the joke-teller laughing at it. A smile, on the other hand, shows that you are happy with how funny your joke is and this can actually make it seem even funnier.

RHYTHM

A good joke has rhythm to it. You need to tune into that rhythm as you are telling the joke. Many shorter jokes have an almost lyrical sound to them. Openings, such as "What do you get..." and "What's the difference..." help us find that rhythm as we launch into the joke.

Rhythm is created by placing emphasis on particular words. In the old classic, *Why* did the *chicken cross* the *road*? we emphasise the important words to give it a lyrical feel and bring the joke to life. We can also use this rhythm to our advantage. In my own variation of this joke I was able to tack two words into the joke, while still maintaining its original rhythm and feel.

Why did the chicken leg cross the road?

To get to the other side-salad.

However, unnecessary words interrupt the rhythm and flow. If you're making up your own jokes, or even remembering one you were told, it's important to strip out all words that are not an integral part of the joke. If you do this you will naturally fall into the rhythm of the joke.

THE DELIVERY

TIMING

One of the quickest ways to become an expert joke-teller is by mastering timing. But on the other hand, getting the timing wrong is one of the easiest ways to kill a joke. If you rush through the setup or drop the punchline in too soon, your joke will fall on its face. However, if you get the timing right, you can have your audience rolling around the floor in laughter.

The trick is to use pauses to build anticipation. Directly before you deliver your punchline, give a dramatic pause. Let your audience wait a few seconds, before BAM! You hit them round the head with your joke. But don't leave them hanging for too long or they might forget what the joke was about.

VARY YOUR VOICE

You should always try to use expression in your voice as you tell a joke, just like when you're reading a story. A dull monotone delivery will not get any laughs. At least, not the kind of laughter that you want. Try varying the volume in different parts of the joke to build tension. Use sound effects wherever you can. Rather than saying, "The siren wailed!" actually make the noise of a siren wailing. This will make the whole process much more entertaining. Even if your audience is not bowled over by your punchline, they will still be entertained and will enjoy the experience.

USE ACTIONS AND GESTURES

Standing there with your arms dangling at your sides as you tell a joke is not going to get you the right kind of laughs either. This might be okay when you're singing a song, but when telling a joke you need to be more animated. Use exaggerated actions and gestures to show what you're saying. As you say, "A guy was driving down the road..." place your hands on an imaginary steering wheel. This adds a visual element to the joke that can get your audience laughing long before the punchline.

PRACTICE MAKES PERFECT

Glancing over this chapter, it can seem like there are an awful lot of things to remember while telling a joke. With practice, these things will come naturally to you. But you do need to practise. Telling jokes to everyone who stands still long enough to listen is one way to do it. Keep a careful eye on the reactions of your audience to see if you can use these skills to get more laughs from the same jokes.

Alternatively, you can practise in front of a mirror. Once you've got the telling of a joke perfected, you can then test it out on unsuspecting passers-by.

It doesn't matter which method you choose ... the only way to become an expert joke-teller is by putting in the time and effort. As with anything, if you keep at it, you'll get better and better.

★ EXERCISE 3 ★

Before you read through this next collection of jokes, choose three more people you can use as guinea pigs. Write their names below (or in your notebook, if you borrowed this from the library!).

Name	Joke 1	Joke 2	Joke 3

Now read through this joke section (plus the previous sections) and select the top three jokes for each person. Write the numbers next to their names. And don't forget to add your favourites to your notebook, as well.

31. How do you stop a dog peeing on the back seat of your car?

Put it in the front seat.

32. Why did the bees go on strike?

They wanted shorter flowers and more honey.

33. What colour is a hiccup?

Burple

34. British Airways have developed an invisible aeroplane. I can't see it taking off.

35. What do you give a naughty horse?

A carrot-y chop!

36. I've got a book all about superglue. I can't put it down.

37. Why did the banana visit the doctor?

It wasn't peeling well.

38. Who was the fastest runner in history?

Adam... He was first in the human race.

39. Why couldn't the pony sing?

It was a little hoarse.

40. What will a cow do if you clean its feet?

Give you a pat on the head

You now have nine jokes to learn, so don't rush it. This time, before we tell the jokes, we will also practise the delivery. When you no longer need the book in front of you, find a mirror in a quiet place. It's probably best not to use public or school toilets, if you can avoid it.

Imagine your reflection is your first guinea pig. Tell their three jokes slowly, one at time, focusing on all the elements we discussed in the previous section. As a reminder, these were:

- Eye contact
- Smile
- Rhythm
- Timing
- Vary your voice
- Use actions and gestures

Keep practising in front of the mirror until you are completely happy with the delivery of the first three jokes, then move on to the next person's jokes.

You are now ready to try out the jokes on your three test subjects. However, it doesn't need to be done right now. If you shake your grandmother awake or interrupt your dad's favourite movie, they're more likely to growl than laugh. Wait for a suitable time. And tell them what you're doing. If you say you're practising telling jokes and ask if you could use them as a guinea pig, they'll probably be happy to help.

REFLECTION

How did that go? Did you improve from last time? Did you find your delivery getting better as you got further down your list? I hope so, because like I said before, practice makes perfect.

Perhaps you didn't get any laughs at all. Or maybe you couldn't find the right time to tell your jokes. If this was the case, don't worry. The next section will help you choose the perfect time and place for joke-telling.

RIGHT TIME, RIGHT PLACE

There's a time and a place for everything. Farting. Picking your nose. Telling jokes. If you don't want people to avoid you, it's important to recognise this.

If you go around telling jokes all the time, people will not only stop laughing at your jokes ... they will stop taking you seriously. And if you pick your nose and fart as well, they'll laugh for all the wrong reasons.

THE PLACE

I won't list all the places where you shouldn't tell jokes. That would fill several books. It's best to focus on the places where you should tell jokes. In fact, it doesn't matter where you are. It's more about what you're doing. Or the fact that you're not doing much. If you try to tell a joke during the middle of a movie or football match, anyone trying to concentrate will get annoyed. For this reason, jokes are best told when nothing else is happening, such as once the movie has finished or during half-time.

Here are some places I have told jokes over the years, but this is by no means an exhaustive list. After all, there are many places I haven't been yet.

- The school playground
- Round a campfire
- On a long walk
- On a long car ride
- When your car has broken down
- On a long bus ride
- When your bus has broken down
- On a long camel ride
- When your camel ~~has broken down~~ is resting
- Bus stops
- Train stations
- Airports
- In a queue
- Underneath the stars
- In Space – Okay, not yet … but maybe one day.

TOPICAL JOKES

As your joke repertoire grows, you'll find that comments and situations often remind you of a joke. You'll hear or see something that will trigger the memory of a particular joke, perhaps long forgotten. It will pop up in your mind, waving its little jokey hands and begging to be told.

When this happens, it's important that you don't just blurt the joke out. First, check that the time and place is right. Also make sure the joke is appropriate for your audience.

If it passes these simple criteria, go ahead and tell your joke. But before you do, you need to let your audience know you are about tell a joke.

PREP TALK

If you launch straight into a joke, you could catch your audience out. They might think you were asking them a serious question or telling them a true story.

RIGHT PLACE, RIGHT TIME

Your audience needs to know that what they are about to hear should not be taken seriously. It's like putting a Bluetooth device into pairing mode – you hold the button down and for the next few moments the device is ready for pairing.

When telling jokes, you say a short preparation phrase or question to get your audience in joke mode. Such as:

- Do you wanna hear a joke?
- Here's a joke...
- That reminds me of a joke...

Each time you give this Prep Talk, your audience goes into pairing – or joking – mode. They know that the next thing you say will be a joke and they get themselves poised and ready to laugh.

RIGHT PLACE, RIGHT TIME

When you give your Prep Talk, the usual response is a quick nod or grunt. They might even sit back eagerly and reach for some popcorn. This is your cue to launch into your joke. If you spend five minutes digging around for your notes or making a quick cup of tea, the moment will pass and you'll have to prep them again.

The Prep Talk also gives your audience an opportunity to decline if they are not in the mood. Usually a stern look or rolling eyes are enough to warn you that it's not an appropriate moment. This isn't a bad thing, since it saves you wasting a perfectly good joke. If someone is not in the mood, even the World's Funniest Joke won't crack a smile.

★ **EXERCISE 4** ★

In this section we will choose jokes to tell in a particular time or place. Each joke below has suggestions for when might be appropriate to tell it. Read through the jokes, remembering to add any beauties to your notebook, then select three situations that you might experience in the next week or two.

Memorise those jokes, practising them in all the usual ways, and wait for each situation (or a similar one) to arise. When it does, remember to prep your audience, then tell your joke.

Hanging out in a busy playground:

41. What's less than a metre long and packed full of kids?

   A school yard

On a car journey:

42. **What breaks every time you use it?**

    A car

Watching motor sports on TV:

43. **What do racing drivers drink before Formula One?**

    Breast milk

A sports game is paused for a foul:

44. **What's it called when a player hits an opponent around the head with a chicken?**

    A fowl

Waiting for your baggage at an airport:

45. It should be easy to find your luggage at the airport. But that's not the case.

Eating your breakfast cereal:

46. Why should you never swim in a bowl of muesli?

There might be a strong currant.

While collecting firewood:

47. How do you make a fire with only one stick?

Make sure it's a match.

Standing in line:

48. Which vegetable likes to wait in line?

A queue-cumber

Waiting for a bus:

49. **When does a bus get wet?**

When it's dew.

Standing around at a wedding:

50. **Did you hear about the cannibal wedding?**

They toasted the bride and groom.

REFLECTION

How did that go? Was it the right time to tell a joke? What did your audience do when you gave your Prep Talk? Were your jokes met with a smile, a laugh or a groan? And did they tell you a joke in response?

   If your audience responded with a joke, you might have found yourself in one of those special joke-telling moments where everyone contributes a joke or ten. If this didn't happen, don't panic ... that's what we're looking at next.

★ JOKE-TELLING ★ SESSIONS

There's nothing wrong with telling a single joke here and there. Like kicking a ball around in the park, it helps you practise your delivery and gain confidence. But if you keep kicking a ball around, sooner or later you will be expected to play a full game of football.

If you keep telling jokes, it won't be long before you find yourself in a joke-telling session. This is when people take it in turns to tell a joke. It starts with a single joke, and everyone laughs, then someone else tells one. Before you know it, everyone is waiting for the next joke.

These moments are the Holy Grail for a joke-lover. Not only do you get to share all the awesome jokes you've been collecting over the years, you might also discover some fresh material to add to your repertoire. Not to mention the fact that they can be heaps of fun!

HAND-PICK YOUR AUDIENCE

Starting a joke-telling session is similar to preparing to tell a single joke. You need to make sure that the time and place are suitable. And you can even use a topical joke as the starting point. The main difference is that you want others to join in too, so you are not single-handedly entertaining the room. One way to avoid putting on a solo show is to consider your audience carefully.

It's a sad fact, but some people just don't like jokes. If you try to initiate a joke-telling session in a room filled with these people, you will not get very far. Other people love jokes but can't ever remember them. These people

won't help you keep the joke session going either, but they're handy if you only have a small repertoire... You can use the same jokes on them every time.

What you're looking for is other joke-tellers. People like yourself who love hearing and sharing jokes. And the better they are at telling jokes, the easier it will be for you. They'll keep the audience laughing while you're trying to think of your next joke. And with one or two other joke-tellers in the session, you'll be able to keep it going for ages, while also picking up plenty more hilarious jokes for your repertoire.

For this reason, it might be a good idea to buy dozens of copies of this book and hand it out to everyone you meet! That way, everyone will know how to tell a joke and you'll constantly find yourself in hilarious joke-telling sessions.

If that's not feasible on your pocket money, here are some of the kinds of people you do and don't want in your joke-telling sessions:

The people you DO want in your joke-telling session:

1. Can't remember jokes but laughs at everything

2. Loves jokes, know hundreds of them and tells them all the time (even when not appropriate)

3. Can only remember one joke but always happy to tell it

4. Very keen, but only has a few jokes in their repertoire – and you've heard them all before

5. Absolutely brilliant joke-teller – will probably be a stand-up comedian one day

The people you DON'T want in your joke-telling session:

1. Hates jokes (and all forms of fun)

2. Knows several jokes but always messes them up by getting the punchline wrong

3. Claims to like jokes but doesn't laugh at anything

4. Tells lots of very inappropriate jokes

5. Takes things personally and is very easily offended

KNOWING WHO'S WHO

It's all very well saying that you should avoid joke-telling situations with some types of people and encourage them with others. The problem is that people are not colour-coded according to their joke-telling ability.

Nor do they wear T-shirts that advertise their joke-orientation, although in certain cases their choice of clothing may well give you a clue!

In general, you'll need to size people up and use your gut instincts. Someone who reads a lot of joke books or who often says funny things would be a good person to include in a joke-telling session. Someone who never laughs at anything might be worth excluding.

The more you tell jokes in a variety of situations and audiences, the better you'll understand who your allies are. A great way to hone your joke-telling skills is to gravitate towards joke-lovers and practise your repertoire on them. A one-on-one joke-telling session with someone who loves telling and hearing jokes is the perfect test-run for new jokes. It's also a brilliant way to build your confidence and get you ready for bigger audiences.

WAITING FOR THE RIGHT MOMENT

Some people are great at starting joke-telling sessions, but you don't have to be. If you're patient, you'll notice that joke-telling opportunities are always popping up. The best time to tell a joke is when someone else has just told one. The ice has already been broken and the audience is warming up.

Even if you're not confident enough to tell the second joke, soon the session will be in full swing and there'll be plenty of pauses between jokes. You just need to indicate that you have a joke to tell, then jump right in and tell it.

CONTINUED PREP TALK

In the last section we talked about the Prep Talk... the short phrase or statement that lets your audience know they are about to hear a joke. Whether you're telling the first joke of the session or the seventeenth, you need to make sure your audience is ready for it. When a session is in full swing, everyone is fairly certain they're about to hear another joke. The role of a Prep Talk at this stage is to let them know they're about to hear a joke from you.

This could mean raising your hand, giving a little wave or leaning forwards, just like you'd do if you wanted to contribute to a conversation. But you can also say a few words to confirm that you're next in the joke queue, such as:

- I've got one...
- Here's another one...
- And what about...
- Have you heard this one?

★ EXERCISE 5 ★

For our next exercise, we're going to initiate a joke-telling session. Think about where and with whom you might do this.

Ideally, there should be three or four other people present. Any fewer and the jokes will dry up quickly or it will become a one-kid show, with you doing all the hard work. Alternatively, if there are too many people, others might be too shy to join in and it really will be a one-kid comedy show.

Who would be a suitable group to start with? It could be your whole family or some of the kids in your class. Whoever you choose, make sure there's at least one other joke-lover in the group, so you'll definitely get some support. This could

mean waiting until your uncle visits or your funny neighbour has dropped in. You could even choose a pre-defined group of people, such as your swimming classmates or your Scout Patrol.

Once you've decided on your group, read through the jokes below and circle the ones that would work well for all those people. Look for suitable gems in the previous sections, too. If any of your guinea pigs are in the group, try to avoid repeating jokes that they've already heard. If your grandmother is part of the group, you might want to hold back on the bum and poo jokes. Or not. It depends on your gran.

This time you don't need to stop at three. In fact, the more the merrier. Often, joke-telling sessions go on until everyone has dried up, so the more you have in your repertoire the better. But don't forget who your audience is. When you start running out of jokes, it can be tempting to dig deep and use some that are more suited to a different audience. This is a sure-fire way to bring the session to an end. It's much better to stop while people are laughing, rather than kill the laughter with an unfunny or offensive joke.

51. My parents bought me a terrible thesaurus. Not only is it terrible, it is also terrible.

52. What happened when a dog went to the flea circus?

It stole the show.

53. Two burglars were caught stealing a calendar. They both got six months.

54. What do you call a person with a tractor on their head?

Dead

55. A father was washing the car with his son. After a while, the son said, "Could you use a sponge instead, please Dad?"

56. Why did Tigger look down the toilet?

He was trying to find Pooh.

57. Waiter, what is this fly doing in my soup?

Front crawl

58. What kind of fur do you get from a hungry lion?

As fur away as possible.

59. I'm friends with twenty-five letters of the alphabet. I don't know why.

60. What do you call a pig with fleas?

Pork scratching

Once you've selected your jokes you need to learn them and be patient. The perfect situation may not arise immediately. Keep running over the jokes in your head while you wait. You could even add new ones from the internet and other joke books. And think about what you'll say to prepare your audience when the time is right. Perhaps one of the following sentences?

- Does anyone know any good jokes?
- Do you want to hear some jokes?
- I've been reading this awesome joke book recently... Do you want to hear some?

Once the joke-telling session is underway, listen carefully to what other people say or do immediately before they tell a joke. Can you detect a pattern? Do people say the same thing every time or mix it up? Do they stop introducing them when the session is in full swing? Other than words, are there particular actions that people do, like standing up or leaning forwards?

REFLECTION

How did that go? Did others join in or did you end up doing all the talking? Did any of your jokes fall flat? If so, was the joke to blame, or was it when, how or to whom it was told? And did you notice any patterns or themes emerging throughout the session? Don't worry if you didn't... that's what we'll be focussing on during the next session.

GO WITH THE FLOW

When telling jokes, it's important to go with the flow. If everyone is telling silly jokes, then pull out your bottom or fart jokes (Just the jokes, though. Keep your bottom and farts to yourself!). But if everyone else is telling cute animal jokes and you chip in with a stinky poo gag, you could disrupt the flow of the session.

It would be like getting driven to school in a World War Two tank. It might sound cool, but most people would stop their vehicles to stare at you in surprise. The traffic would be so bad you probably wouldn't get to school on time.

Likewise, a mis-timed or inappropriate joke will disrupt the flow of a joke session. People might be shocked into silence. They may even laugh at *you*, rather than at the joke. This is not a great place to be. Not only are you likely to have killed the joke session, but you might find that people will stop telling jokes around you at all.

IN THE BEGINNING

If someone starts off by telling a knock-knock joke, it's a good idea to follow it up with another knock-knock joke. The next person will probably continue with another, and for a while, it will be a knock-knock-only zone.

Don't panic. You won't be trapped in a knock-knock nightmare forever. You usually find that joke-telling sessions start with a specific category or theme, then broaden out as time goes on and people dig deeper.

I was at a barbecue one weekend where someone told a name joke, starting "What do you call a girl who...". After a short chuckle, I followed it up with some similar name jokes from my old repertoire. Someone else threw in another name joke or two, then the session morphed into any old jokes that people could think of. Rather than getting too involved, contributing heaps of my own jokes, I took a more observational role, enjoying seeing where the session ended up. It only lasted around five minutes and, even though we moved away from name jokes, all the other jokes were of a similar length and tone.

This is what makes joke-telling sessions so unique and awesome. They can take on a life of their own, with each joke naturally flowing on to another, taking the session in a new and exciting direction. Like fingerprints, no two joke sessions are ever the same. You'll find that you contribute a different selection of your repertoire every time you're involved in one, depending on how the session starts, the other people who are there and how you're feeling at the time.

STEERING THE SHIP

The captain of a large ship could turn the wheel so slowly that the passengers wouldn't even notice a change in direction. The same captain has the ability to make everyone spill their drinks.

This is how it is with jokes. An expert joke-teller can steer the session in any direction they choose. When one category or style of jokes dries up, they can lead everyone in a different direction. This is done by choosing a joke to act as a stepping stone to a new collection. One that was similar to the last joke but that can lead onto something different.

For example, if everyone is telling cute animal jokes, you could tell an animal poo joke. Then, instead of following it up with another animal joke, you drop in another poo joke.

The next thing you know, everyone is telling all the poo jokes they know, without even realising you led them there on purpose.

It doesn't even have to be you that comes up with the stepping-stone joke. You could take a theme from the previous joke that someone else told and run with that theme. If someone mentions a dog, that could lead into a different dog joke. Or if someone tells a longer joke, it might be time to bust out that fiive-minute gag.

FIND YOUR FLOW

Telling jokes within a particular category or based on a particular theme helps you find your own rhythm and flow.

At this stage in my career, I've written more than one thousand original jokes, but when someone asks me to tell me a joke, my

mind goes blank. There are simply too many options. However, if I think of a particular theme, such as dog or bum jokes (or perhaps dog-bum jokes!), they start rolling off the tongue. Once I've started, more and more jokes spring to mind. Before I know it, ten minutes have passed and my wife is glaring at me.

Despite the glares, finding your flow is a beautiful thing. You're lost in the moment with jokes pouring out of you. Everyone is laughing. It's every joke-teller's Happy Place. But while you're there, remember to stay mindful and aware of those around you. It's easy to get so lost inside your mind as you hunt for the perfect next joke that you stop observing your audience. This makes you less alert to shifts in mood or unintended reactions. You should also listen to other people's jokes and the way they're received to stay with the flow. Plus, you'll need to remember those gems, so you can add them to your notebook later on.

★ EXERCISE 6 ★

In this exercise, we will start organising our jokes into categories or themes. That way, when we hear a joke in a particular theme or style, we'll be able to go with the flow, hopefully turning an off-hand joke into a longer joke-telling session.

Read the jokes from four different categories below. If there any you like, add that category to your joke notebook and start to fill it with the best examples you can find.

You'll notice that the fifth joke in each collection is different from the other four. These jokes could all be used as stepping stones to help steer a joke session in a different direction.

KNOCK KNOCK JOKES

61. Knock, knock...

Who's there?

Ewan...

Ewan who?

Ewan me need to talk.

62. Knock, knock...

Who's there?

Sez...

Sez who?

Sez me!

63. Knock, knock...

Who's there?

Howie...

Howie who?

I'm fine, thanks. You?

64. Knock, knock...

Who's there?

Noah...

Noah who?

Noah place where I can hear some decent jokes?

65. The person who invented knock-knock jokes deserves a No-Bell prize.

CHICKEN JOKES

66. Why did the chicken cross the playground?

> To get to the other slide.

67. Why did the robo-chicken cross the road?

> To get to the other cyborg.

TINK

68. Why did the rubber chicken cross the road?

She wanted to stretch her legs.

69. Why did the bully cross the road?

He was a chicken.

70. What did the farmer say when he took roll call in the hen house?

"Just chicken!"

DOCTOR DOCTOR JOKES

71. Doctor, doctor, every time I drink coffee, I get a stabbing pain in my eye!

    Try taking the spoon out first.

72. Doctor, doctor, I think I'm turning into a pirate!

    Open wide and say "Arrrrgh!"

73. Doctor, doctor, I just swallowed a golf ball.

Yes, I can see it's gone down a fair-way.

74. Doctor, doctor, every day I seem to double in size.

I think you need a shrink.

75. What did the doctor say when his daughter had a tantrum in his waiting room?

"I'm losing my patients!"

NAME JOKES

76. What do you call a girl with a moustache?

    Tash

77. What do you call a boy who swallowed a rabbit?

    Warren

78. What do you call a boy standing in a bucket?

Phil

79. What do you call a girl with a frog on her head?

Lily

80. What do you call a fish that's lost an eye?

A fsh

Now look at the categories below. Do you know any jokes that would fit into them? If so, add the category to your joke notebook and start collecting. See if you can add at least three jokes to each new category to get yourself started.

- Animal Jokes
- Funny Book Titles
- Holidays
- School
- Numbers
- Spelling
- Jokes for Little Kids

REFLECTION

How did it go? Were there lots of categories you wanted to add? Or not so many? And was it easy to find new jokes for every category? If it wasn't, don't panic... In the next section we will focus on how to build your repertoire.

BUILD YOUR REPERTOIRE

By this point, both your joke notebook and your head should be filling with jokes. There should be a variety of jokes in your collection, suitable for different audiences and situations.

This is great! But it's only the beginning. A good joke repertoire is constantly growing and evolving. New jokes should join the party all the time, building that repertoire. Older jokes will be dropping off, too, unused and forgotten. If you want to be an expert joke-teller, you need to learn more new jokes than you forget old ones. This way, over the years, you will gain a vast mental collection of jokes.

LISTEN TO OTHER JOKE-TELLERS

When you share jokes from your repertoire, your audience will share theirs too. If you're among other experts, these jokes will have been honed and perfected over the years. This is a great way to build your repertoire. Listen carefully as each joke is being told. If you like the sound of it and it makes you laugh, try to commit it to memory. If you can remember nothing else, memorise the punchline. You can always work backwards to figure out the rest of the joke.

Don't be afraid to ask someone to tell a joke again, either. Joke-tellers love it when people enjoy their jokes. And they will be only too happy to retell their favourites. After all, that joke made it into their repertoire for a reason.

When you get home, jot any new jokes that you heard down in your notebook. And run through them in your head until they become part of your own repertoire.

READ JOKE BOOKS

Joke books are a great source of new jokes. If you own the book, you won't even need to add the joke to your notebook. Just circle any that make you laugh and remember to flick through it occasionally to commit them to memory. If you add a joke book to your birthday and Christmas wish list each year, before long you'll have a whole library of joke books to flick through.

Here are a few I recommend:

- The **I'm Joking** series *by Tom E. Moffatt* – Okay, I'm biased! But I've tried to come up with completely original jokes, so this is a great place to find jokes that no one has heard before.

- **Awesome Jokes that every 5/6/7/8/9-Year-Old Should Know** *by Mat Waugh* – These books are great for finding those perfect jokes for your audience's age level.

- **The Big Book of Silly Jokes for Kids** *by Carol P Roman* – A huge book crammed with more than 800 jokes.

- **Laugh-out-loud Jokes for Kids** *by Rob Elliott* – This book has been around for a while but is very popular, especially in the USA.

- **Silly Jokes for Silly Kids** by *Silly Willy* – Another classic that is guaranteed to get a laugh or two.
- **Roald Dahl's joke books** – All these are worth a read, especially if you like Roald Dahl's stories.
- **The Bumper Book of Very Silly Jokes** *published by Macmillan Children's Books* – A good place to find lots of the old classics.

This is just an appetiser. There are more amazing joke books published every day. But be sure to read the customer reviews before you buy, because not every joke book is created equal, and readers are the first to point out if something's no good.

SEARCH THE INTERNET

The internet can be an even better resource than books for building your repertoire. This is because you can use it to fill specific gaps you may have in your collection. Perhaps you're interested in finding some political humour for an older audience, or some bone jokes for your dog. Whatever it may be, you can type it into Google and see what comes up. You can also search for longer jokes, one-liners, shaggy dog tales... whatever it is you would like to add to your repertoire.

There is a wide range of quality on the internet, so you'll have to sieve a lot of silt to find the gold nuggets. You also need to watch out for inappropriate content. Don't forget that one way to filter this out is to add the words 'for kids' to your search.

My website – www.TomEMoffatt.com/jokes – contains hundreds of jokes in more than forty categories, so this would be a good place to start. Other great joke sites are:

- www.funology.com/funology-jokes-and-riddles
- jokes.boyslife.org
- www.rd.com/jokes/kids
- www.ducksters.com/jokes
- www.wickeduncle.co.uk/jokes
- jokes4us.com/miscellaneousjokes/schooljokes/kidjokes
- frugalfun4boys.com/hilarious-jokes-for-kids
- www.coolkidfacts.com/jokes-for-kids
- www.fourkidz.com/home
- www.scarymommy.com/best-jokes-for-kids

YOUTUBE

YouTube is also a great place to find jokes, because some jokes are better heard than read. Plus, you get to witness both good and bad examples of joke-telling. It's hard to find YouTube channels that consistently post jokes, since most of the quality productions are one-off videos. But there are lots of great 'Try-not-to-laugh' challenge videos for kids.

However, if you subscribe to my YouTube channel – *Tom E. Moffatt's Write Laugh* – you'll get to hear me telling original jokes every month.

The Joke Site is another good channel to subscribe to. It has tons of existing collections and regularly adds new material.

MAINTAIN YOUR EXISTING COLLECTION

Searching for new jokes is a great way to grow your repertoire, but you also need to undertake regular maintenance on your existing collection. Otherwise, the new additions will be the only jokes you can remember.

Remember to flick through your notebook from time to time to re-familiarise yourself with your repertoire. Maybe you could run through all the jokes in your head, seeing how many you can remember. That way, when a joke-telling situation arises, you'll be ready to access your repertoire and tell some of your favourite jokes. When you've done this enough, you'll find that the best jokes stick around. You'll be able to recount them without much thought, and your telling of them will become better and better.

Eventually, after years of collecting, your joke repertoire will become so big it will be impossible to remember them all. This doesn't matter. Some jokes will lie dormant for many years, before a comment or situation triggers your memory.

BUILD YOUR REPERTOIRE

This can help you become funnier in everyday life, not just joke-telling sessions, because who doesn't love a well-told, topical joke?

And don't be afraid to remove a joke from your collection if it's not working. If no one laughs at a particular joke or if it consistently causes offence, just cross it out and stop using it. There are plenty more fsh in the C.

★ EXERCISE 7 ★

In this section we will practise using research to fill gaps in your repertoire. There could be many reasons why you need a specific joke.

Perhaps you're doing a project at school and want to lighten things up. Or maybe you want to entertain people at a particular time of year. Christmas and Halloween are joke-telling seasons, so it makes sense to include them as categories in your collection. Here are some jokes you could add to those categories:

CHRISTMAS JOKES

81. What do you get if you swallow Christmas decorations?

Tinsillitis

82. Which spies only come out at Christmas?

Minspies

83. What did Santa pay for his sleigh?

Nothing, it was on the house.

84. Why are there only twenty-five letters in the alphabet at Christmas time?

Noel

85. What do you call Father Christmas when he's not wearing undies?

St. Knicker-less

HALLOWEEN JOKES

86. Who collects nectar from dead flowers?

Zombees

87. What comes out of your nose on Halloween?

The bogeyman

88. Why didn't the skeleton eat its Halloween candy?

It didn't have the stomach for it.

89. Where do ghosts prefer to trick-or-treat?

Dead-ends

90. Why did the sausage dress up as a monster?

It was a Hallowiener.

EXERCISE 7

There are lots of places to find specific jokes. You can flick through joke books, trawl through Google or binge-watch YouTube videos. Pick the method that suits you best, then try to find a funny joke for each of the following categories:

- A bum joke
- A funny book title/author name
- A one-liner
- A joke suitable for a five-year-old
- A long joke

Once you've found all five of the jokes above, add them to your repertoire. Then look through your collection to see if there are any gaps, such as missing themes or types of jokes. Using the same method that you used above, try to fill those gaps by adding one or two jokes to each category.

REFLECTION

How did you go? Did you find lots of fine new specimens for your collection? Was it easy to find specific jokes or did you get lost in the rabbit warren of online jokes? Were any categories harder to find than others?

I personally think it's hard to find really good long jokes, yet they are arguably the most valuable jokes in your collection. Which is why we're going to focus on them next.

★ LONGER JOKES ★

Longer jokes give you a chance to shine as a joke-teller. Like a thousand-year-old coin or an ultra-rare Pokémon card, they should be the pride of your collection.

They enable you to take centre stage for longer and provide the opportunity to use more actions and sound effects. You can also add in your own details and language choices, as long as you remember the key points of the story and the punchline.

That said, it also requires more effort to learn the jokes properly and to deliver them well. And it can be harder to keep a lot of them in your mental repertoire. Don't let this put you off. You should always be on the lookout for new long jokes to add to your collection. When you find one, you'll need to study it and practise it before it becomes a part of your repertoire. Here are a few tips to help you remember and deliver longer jokes.

MEMORISE THE PUNCHLINE

The most important part of the joke is the punchline. This is also the only part that needs to be memorised word for word. Run it over in your mind several times and practise saying it out loud, finding the right rhythm and intonation. Once you've memorised it, see if you can unpack it. What is it that makes this punchline funny (or not!)?

UNDERSTAND THE IMPORTANT ELEMENTS

A punchline is not funny on its own. It's only funny in contrast with the setup. Analyse the setup carefully, trying to figure out which elements of the joke must be included for the punchline to work. Some jokes only work with a particular character, such as a young girl or a panda. Some would work with any character, provided they are in a specific situation. You need to work out which details are essential in order to tell a longer joke well.

SUMMARISE THE JOKE

Once you understand the important elements of the joke, see if you can summarise it in a few key sentences. Try to get the joke down to its bare bones, the crucial parts that make it work. This is what you can write in your joke notebook. It's also what you need to run through in your mind when you are first learning a long joke.

145

ADD DETAILS

When you understand the structure of the
joke, you need to add the details back in. You
can do this using the language that you first
heard or read. Or you can add your own flavour
to it, make the joke yours. Some people like to
personalise a joke, making it about their own
life, as though it actually happened to them.
You can also tailor a joke towards your specific
audience, if you already have one in mind.

    This is the point where you need to
practise your joke. You can run
through it silently at first,
perhaps while on the way
to school or at the
supermarket.
Then, once
you're confident
that you know
the joke, you

need to practise it out loud. To avoid making people think you've gone bonkers, you might want to do this alone in your bedroom.

ADD ACTIONS AND SOUND EFFECTS

While you practise your joke out loud, see if you can make the story funnier or more visual. Throw in actions and sound effects wherever you can. This keeps the audience engaged and entertained, even before you hit them with the punchline.

Try to build up the actions as you work through the joke. If you start out with arms swinging and voice wailing, your audience won't know what hit them. Give them a few smaller actions first, such as walking down the street or licking an ice cream. Then, when you have them engaged, pick up the pace, saving your big guns until the climax of the joke.

DELIVERING THE PUNCHLINE

Even with all your screaming and jumping up and down, the punchline is still the most important part of the joke. Deliver it carefully and clearly. If your audience don't quite hear what you said the whole joke will be lost, so make sure you say it loudly enough, too. Often, a pause of several seconds can build anticipation and increase its impact. And don't forget to make eye contact and smile while you say it.

EXAMPLE JOKE – BALLOON BOY

Before we head into the next exercise section, let's have a go at breaking a longer joke down together. Read this joke first, then we'll go through all the elements above, one at a time.

Balloon Boy sneaked out of his balloon school and started ballooning around in the balloon playground. When no one was looking he fiddled with a valve on the side of the balloon building. Suddenly the entire balloon school went "TTTHHHHHBBBRRRRRRRR RRRRrrrrrrrrrrrrrr!" (Use hands to show it getting smaller.)

Suddenly the balloon headmaster appeared and rushed over to Balloon Boy, shouting,

"What the ballooning heck do you think you're doing, you ballooning imbecile!?"

Balloon Boy knew he was in serious trouble now. He looked around frantically for a way out when he spotted a valve on the balloon headmaster's stomach.

Without saying a word, he reached out and pressed the valve. The balloon headmaster went, "TTTHHHHHBBBRRRRRRRRRRRR RRRrrrrrrrrrrrrrrrr!" (Use actions again.)

Balloon Boy stood there all alone. He was in such trouble now! He hung his head and started to cry. Through his balloon tears he spotted a valve on his own stomach. Without giving it too much thought he pushed the valve. "TTTHHHHHBBBRRRRRRRRRRRR RRRrrrrrrrrrrrrrrrr!"

Moments later a balloon

ambulance came ballooning towards the scene. BALLOOOOON, BALLOOOOON, BALLOOOOON!

Balloon paramedics rushed out and carefully carried Balloon Boy and the balloon headmaster into the balloon ambulance. As the ambulance went ballooning towards the balloon hospital, the paramedics began pumping the two balloon people back up. Fffft, ffft, ffft, ffft!

When Balloon Boy began to come around, he saw his balloon headmaster lying next to him, getting bigger by the moment.

The balloon headmaster turned to Balloon Boy with a disappointed look on his balloon face. Then he said, "Sonny, you let the school down and you let me down. But worst of all, you let yourself down!"

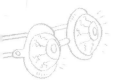
PUNCHLINE

The headmaster says, "You let the school down and you let me down. But worst of all, you let yourself down!"

It needs to be clear that the headmaster is saying this. Whether or not he calls the boy Sonny is up to you. It isn't an essential detail.

UNDERSTAND THE IMPORTANT ELEMENTS

The punchline is a common phrase that you might hear at school. What makes it funny here is that the balloon boy did literally let all those things down. Therefore, for the punchline to work, the balloon boy needs to let the school, the headmaster and himself down.

However, the fact that the character is a boy is not an essential part of the joke. You could make it a girl, if you like, but I used Balloon Boy because I liked the alliteration.

SUMMARY

- Balloon boy is at a balloon school.
- He lets the air out of the school.
- He lets the air out of the school principal.
- He lets the air out of himself.
- Paramedics pump them both back up.
- The principal says, "You let the school down and you let me down. But worst of all, you let yourself down!"

DETAILS

Exactly how you describe all those elements of the joke is entirely up to you. You can exchange Balloon Boy for Balloon Girl. You can also change what the balloon child is doing at or outside school. You can make the headmaster say things more specific to your school. You can do anything you like, provided your joke still contains all the important elements.

I like the excessive use of the word 'balloon', but this too is non-essential, provided the listener knows that we are dealing with balloon people. The details are yours to change to suit your style of joke-telling.

ACTIONS AND SOUND EFFECTS

One thing I love about this joke is the fact that it lends itself to the use of actions and sound effects. The punchline itself isn't utterly brilliant, but the whole joke can be pretty funny, if told well. I've included a few possible actions in the joke, but there are many more possibilities. You could show the actions of the misbehaving balloon child. Or perhaps the paramedics could use a hand pump to blow them both back up. The more animated you make the joke, the better. And, generally speaking, each of your actions can be accompanied by some sort of sound effect.

PUNCHLINE

Rehearse the punchline until it flows out of you without any thought. Can you deepen your voice to make it sound like the headmaster? Can you make him sound weak, like he's on his deathbed? Practise to see what sounds best, but remember that the most important thing is that everyone can hear you clearly, so don't overdo the use of sound effects if they get in the way of understanding.

PRACTICE

Now you understand the joke, you need to practise telling it. Whether you change the details or keep them more or less the same, run through the story several times in your head, making sure you include all the key elements. Once you know the story, say it out loud in front of a mirror to work on the delivery. Ideally, you want to get to the stage when you can retell the joke without having to give it too much thought.

TEST IT OUT

When you can recount the joke seamlessly and are happy with how it sounds, try telling it to someone. As you're doing so, notice how your audience reacts. Are the actions and sound effects met with laughter or horror? Is the story tight enough, or was there a lull in the middle? Did they find the punchline funny? These things can help you improve the way you deliver the joke next time.

★ EXERCISE 8 ★

This time we're going to choose a suitable audience for a specific joke. Read through the ten longer jokes in this section and circle the ones that resonate with you.

When telling long jokes, it's especially important that you love your material. If you don't enjoy the joke and find it funny, neither will your audience.

Once you've circled all the jokes you like, choose your absolute favourite and write its title in the box below. Now think about three other people who would also like that joke and add their names in the spaces provided.

Joke Title	
Audience 1	
Audience 2	
Audience 3	

91. <u>A Bad Night</u>

I was lying in bed the other night when the doorbell rang. Half asleep, I got out of bed, put on my dressing gown and opened the front door. There, standing on the doorstep, was a six-foot-tall cockroach. Before I had time to shut the door it leapt on me, punching and kicking with all six of its legs. All I could do was cover my head with my arms while it laid into me. After several minutes it got tired and scuttled away. I closed the door and staggered back to my bed.

A few hours later the doorbell rang again. This time I was half delirious. Without thinking, I rushed to the door and opened it. The cockroach was back and all I could do was yelp as it pounced on me and began pummelling me once again. This time it kept going for a full ten minutes and I was so exhausted I couldn't even make it back to my bed. I slept right there on the floor in the hallway.

The next day I was in so much pain I took myself straight to the doctor's. My heart sank as I saw the size of the queue coming out of the surgery door, but I stood at the end of it, patiently waiting. The next moment, the doctor walked out of this office and looked along the queue. When he saw me he waved and said, "You, come with me."

I followed him into his office.

"Let me guess," the doctor began, "you were awoken by the doorbell in the middle of the night and a giant cockroach beat you up!"

"How do you know that?" I asked.

"There's a nasty bug going round!"

92. **_Action Cat_**

A guy was driving down the street one morning when a cat ran out in front of his car. He didn't even have time to brake before he hit it. He pulled over and went to have a look. The cat was lying in the middle of the road, completely dead. He looked at the cat's collar and there was an address written on it. It was only a few doors away, so the man took a deep breath and rang the bell.

A lady answered the door in her dressing gown.

"I'm sorry to bother you," the man said, "but I think I just killed your cat."

"Why, what did it look like?" the woman asked.

The man did this: (Loll your head to the side, roll your eyes back and stick your tongue out, as though dead.)

"No, what did it look like before you hit it?"

So the guy did this: (Hold your hands up beside your face, open your eyes wide and give a startled expression.)

93. <u>Cold Water</u>

A Girl Guide offered to mow the lawn for a poor old man who lived in her village. When she arrived at his house, the man was so grateful he invited her in for a cup of tea and a cookie.

As she ate her cookie, the girl noticed a shiny substance coating her plate. When the old man saw her staring at it, he said, "Sorry, dear, it's as clean as cold water could get it."

When she'd finished mowing the lawn the old man invited her in again for a sandwich. This time, she noticed, not only was there a shiny substance, it also had hard patches of dried egg on it.

"I'm so sorry," the old man said again. "It's as clean as cold water could get it."

The girl smiled politely and finished her sandwich. When she went to leave, an old dog, that had been asleep on its bed, stood up and blocked the doorway, its teeth bared as it growled at her.

The man waved his walking stick at the dog. Then he shouted, "Cold Water … get back in your basket!"

94. <u>A Couple of Words</u>

A man was asked to say a couple of words at his friend's funeral. He stood up nervously and said, "Special Offer."

The friend's widow wiped a tear from her eye.

"Thank you," she said, "that means a Great Deal!"

95. <u>Good Dog</u>

It turns out that my sister is allergic to our little pet dog, so we have to get rid of her. If you know a loving home that can take her in, please let me know. She is eight years old, house trained, loves running around the garden, and always does her homework.

96. <u>Bad Maths</u>

A school boy fell off his chair during a maths lesson and sprained his finger. The teacher grabbed a first-aid kit and applied a splint. Only after she'd finished did they realise that she'd put it on the wrong finger.

"I'm sorry," the teacher said, looking rather embarrassed.

"That's okay, Miss," the boy said. "You were only off by one digit."

97. <u>A Terrible Storm</u>

We had a terrible storm the other night with torrential rain, booming thunder and crashing lightning. My little brother watched through the window for hours ... until I thought, "I should probably let him in."

98. <u>**A Long Wait**</u>

Once upon a time there was a prince who talked too much. He would just talk and talk and talk without ever listening.

His fairy godmother got so fed up that she cast a spell that meant he could only speak a single word each year. If he didn't speak for the entire year, the following year he could say two words.

One day the prince fell in love with a beautiful princess from a neighbouring realm. He waited a whole year just to be able to say her name. But by then he was deeply in love, so he refrained from speaking for three more years so he could tell her he loved her. But by the time the three years were up he decided he wanted to marry her, so he waited for four more years.

Finally, after eight years, he took her to the most romantic spot in the kingdom, got down on one knee and said, "Eleanor, I love you! Will you marry me?"

And the princess said, "Pardon?"

99. _Noisy Dogs_

Arnav walks to school with his mum every day. When they pass the house next door, their young Doberman starts barking. Further up the street a small terrier growls. There are three poodles in the house on the corner that yap away. Arnav hates dogs and gets more and more nervous about going to school each day.

To make Arnav feel better, his dad decides to walk him to school. As they pass the Doberman it just lies down and stares at them. The terrier doesn't even leave its kennel. When they get to the house on the corner the poodles don't make a peep.

"Wow, Dad!" Arnav says. "How do you do it?"

"It's simple," Dad says. "I'm wearing my Hush Puppies!"

100. <u>Like Lightning</u>

A young boy was doing some handiwork with his father. When it came to putting a picture on the wall the father said, "I'll do this one... You're like lightning with a hammer!"

The boy said, "Wow, is that cos I'm so fast?"

"No, it's because you never strike the same place twice!"

Now use the following stages to break your chosen joke down, just like we did in the previous section.

- Start by understanding and memorising the punchline.
- Think about all the crucial elements that build up to that punchline.
- Jot down a brief summary in your notebook.
- In your head, start adding the details back in, either keeping them the same as the original joke or adding your own flavour.
- Once you've run through the joke in your head several times, practise telling it out loud in front of the mirror.
- Add in actions and sound effects to bring it to life.

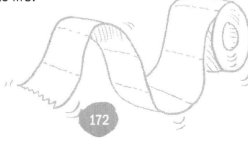

WHOOPEE CUSHION

When you know the joke well and are happy with how it sounds, you are ready to tell it. Track down one of the people on your list, make sure the time is right, then tell them your joke. Don't be tempted to tell it to all three people at once. It's much better to do it one at a time to give yourself the opportunity to learn and improve.

While you're telling your joke, watch the other person carefully. Are they engaged throughout? Do they smile and laugh at the right places? Once you're done, you could even ask them what they thought of it. This kind of feedback is crucial to becoming an expert joke-teller.

REFLECTION

How did that go? Did you manage to get through the joke smoothly and include all the necessary information? Did you remember to use actions and sound effects? If so, move on to the next person on your list. If not, practise in front of the mirror until you're ready to try again.

Telling longer jokes is a great way to lift your repertoire up to the next level and to look like an expert joke-teller. Go through the other long jokes, learning and practising them in the same way.

★ THE BEGINNING ★

Congratulations on making it to the end of the book. You now have all the tools and strategies you need to be an expert joke-teller, but please don't stop here.

You are only at the beginning of your journey.

When you learn the piano, you spend hours each week practising, honing your skills. If you keep up your practice for years, or even decades, you may one day be good enough to be a concert pianist. But that doesn't mean you'll stop practising. You'll then be playing at the top level, compared against other concert pianists, so you'll still have to build your repertoire and continue to improve every day.

It's the same with joke-telling. Now that you can tell jokes well and know heaps of hilarious ones, people will expect it of you. When a joke-telling situation arises, all eyes may turn your way, waiting for you to entertain the group.

To be ready for this moment, you need to keep practising your jokes whenever the opportunity arises. And continue to collect jokes, constantly adding to and refreshing your repertoire.

One way to regularly receive fresh jokes is to join my mailing list. I will email you a brand-new collection of jokes every month and will also let you know when I have a new joke book coming out.

Go to TomEMoffatt.com/keepjoking to subscribe now.

But simply collecting new jokes is not enough. You need to continue to love jokes and to share them whenever the opportunity presents itself. Your love and enjoyment will shine through, so even if you fumble a few words or drop a punchline, your audience won't mind. They'll enjoy the experience anyway.

So, go forth and tell jokes to anyone who will listen.

And share them with me, too. I'm always on the lookout for awesome jokes! If you think you know the best joke ever, please send it to me at TomE@writelaugh.com. Not only will I jot it down in my notebook, but I might also add it to the Readers' Favourites section of my next joke book.

I always like to finish on a joke, so here's a final one for you...

101.   Do you want to hear two short jokes and one long joke?

Okay ... joke, joke, joooooooooooooooke.

ALSO BY TOM E. MOFFATT

THE JOKE COLLECTORS NOTEBOOK

Heard a funny one-liner in the playground?

Found some hilarious jokes online?

Jot them all down in the *Joke Collector's Notebook*, complete with 100+ illustrated jokes, fun challenges and handy tips on finding and telling jokes.

For a FREE Word document version, go to:

www.TomEMoffatt.com/notebook

CREATE YOUR OWN KNOCK-KNOCK JOKES

Want to knock bad jokes on the head?

This book breaks down the joke-writing process into easy to follow steps:

- Learn everything there is to know about knock-knock jokes
- Discover how to write knock-out punchlines
- Follow the tips and prompts to create your own brilliant jokes

Packed with 100+ hilarious examples and 1000+ possibilities for your own creations, this book will make you so funny your friends will be knocking your door down for more jokes.

I'M JOKING

&

I'M SERIOUSLY JOKING

Bored of hearing the same old jokes?

Me too!

That's why I filled *I'm Joking & I'm Seriously Joking* with 1000+ original laugh-out-loud jokes for kids. From barking mad dog jokes to stinky poo gags, these jokes are so fresh and funny that people will think you made them up yourself. Which is fine, as long as you remember to buy me a doughnut when you're a world-famous comedian.

BONKERS SHORT STORIES

These hilarious, action-packed stories transport you to a world where mind-swapping is possible. But be warned: Looking in the mirror will never be the same again.

Volume One: MIND-SWAPPING MADNESS

A boy in a fly's body. A toad waiting to be kissed. Horses that know Morse code and aliens who hijack children's bodies. Has everyone gone bonkers?

Volume Two: BODY-HOPPING HYSTERICS

Not all superpowers are a good thing. Especially NOT if your mum has them. Or if they're fuelled by embarrassment. And what if you can't find your way back home?

FREE SHORT STORY COLLECTION

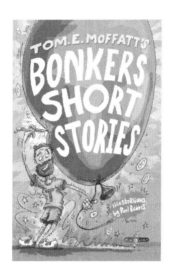

Go to www.TomEMoffatt.com/books to download my free collection of Bonkers Short Stories. You'll also receive monthly newsletters containing brand new jokes and news of my upcoming releases.

ABOUT THE
AUTHOR

Tom E. Moffatt is serious about writing jokes.
He's not allowed to watch Netflix, listen to a
podcast or read a book until he's come up with
at least three new jokes that day. If you see him
laughing as he fills his supermarket trolley or
drives around his home town of Rotorua, don't
worry. He's not laughing at you. He probably
just came up with a hilarious new joke.

For more information, original jokes and lots
more silliness, visit his home on the web:
www.TomEMoffatt.com. But be warned: it may
contain nuts!

RESOURCES

"Joke." kids.britannica.com. Merriam-Webster, 2020.
Web. Accessed January 2020.

"Joke." Wikipedia, The Free Encyclopedia. Wikipedia,
The Free Encyclopedia. Accessed January 2020.

"How to Tell a Joke." wikiHow, www.wikihow.com/Tell-a-
Joke. Accessed January 2020.

"How to Tell a Joke." The Telegraph,
www.telegraph.co.uk/good-news/seven-seas/how-to-
tell-a-joke. Accessed January 2020.

"You want to be funny?"
www.westsidetoastmasters.com/article_reference/
how_to_tell_jokes. Accessed January 2020.

"How to Teach Kids to Tell a Joke." Care.com,
www.care.com/c/stories/5230/how-to-teach-kids-to-
tell-a-joke. Accessed January 2020.

"How to Tell Jokes Like a Pro." The Guardian,
www.theguardian.com/lifeandstyle/2014/jun/19/how-
tell-jokes-like-pro-leah-green. Accessed January 2020.

ACKNOWLEDGEMENTS

Thank you to everyone who submitted jokes via Facebook, my website or in person during school visits. Apologies if I didn't manage to catch your name and put it in the word cloud, but thanks for sharing... you've made me, and hopefully many other people, laugh!

Baillie Farrington
Matilda Soul-Flower Emma Van Paige
Stylez Rawiri Isaiah Hoani
Pedro G Kaniah Layla Zac Sarah
Florence Marliese Ben Wilcock
Bailee Dylana Bunt
Isaac Simian Victoria Jo Nate Weston
Danuji Dylan
Greg W Ethen Harmony Maraea Tyler Grant Lewis Dailly
Lily Julian Tezza Annabel
Leah VDE Alexander Taling Vinny Higman
Jet Brody Prowse Esther Hannaford
Cloe Ben Brundish
Lily Bloomfield Tessis Debnam
Chris Dennis
Magdalena

Thanks also to those who took my survey, especially the senior students at Mamaku School. Your feedback (and jokes) helped me put this book together.

Lastly, thanks to my wife, Sarah, and my three daughters, for putting up with my joke-telling without too many groans or eye-rolls. Life without you guys just wouldn't be funny!

Made in the USA
Las Vegas, NV
12 October 2022